READ A POEM — WRITE A POEM

Poems compiled with notes by Wes Magee

Blackwell Education

This selection copyright © 1989 Wes Magee

First published 1989
Reprinted 1991

Basil Blackwell Ltd
108 Cowley Road
Oxford OX4 1JF
UK

British Library Cataloguing in Publication Data

Read a poem, write a poem.
   1. Poetry – For schools.
   I. Magee, Wes
   808.1

ISBN 0–631–16333–6
ISBN 0–631–90281–3 Pbk

Illustrated by David Parkins, Shoo Rayner and Martin Ursell
Typeset in 14pt Plantin
by Columns of Reading
Printed and bound in Hong Kong
by Wing King Tong Co. Ltd

CONTENTS

Every child's answer to that telephone query from a distant relative

'Are you growing up fast?'

'Yes, I've just hit the ceiling.
Now I've gone through the roof
And at present I'm kneeling
To hear what you're saying,
With my legs through the door,
One arm through the window,
My chin on the floor
And my feet in the roadway,
Which are causing a worry
With a traffic jam stretching
For ten miles through Surrey.

So I'd better ring off . . .

Bye.'

Trevor Harvey

O witches and wizards

O witches and wizards, where have you been?
  We've been to a party for old Hallowe'en.

A Hallowe'en party! O what did you eat?
  Spiced turnip lanterns and hot cauldron treat.

And after the eating what games did you play?
  Old Spells, Hokey-Pokey, and Scare-Them-Away.

And after the games did you dance all together?
  We danced like the North wind in rough, stormy
  weather.

O witches and wizards, what else did you do?
  Ah, that is our secret. We cannot tell you.

Cynthia Mitchell

Rabbiting on

Where did you go?
Oh . . . nowhere much.

What did you see?
Oh . . . rabbits and such.

Rabbits? What else?
Oh . . . a rabbit hutch.

What sort of rabbits?
What sort? Oh . . . small.

What sort of hutch?
Just a hutch, that's all.

But what did it look like?
Like a rabbit hutch.

Well, what was in it?
Small rabbits and such.

I worried about you
While you were gone.

*Why don't you stop
Rabbiting on?*

Kit Wright

The first men on Mercury

– We come in peace from the third planet.
  Would you take us to your leader?

>   – Bawr stretter! Bawr. Bawr. Stretterhawl?

– This is a little plastic model
  of the solar system, with working parts.
  You are here and we are there and we
  are now here with you, is this clear?

>   – Gawl horrop. Bawr. Abawrhannahanna!

– Where we come from is blue and white
  with brown, you see we call the brown
  here 'land', the blue is 'sea', and the white
  is 'clouds' over land and sea, we live
  on the surface of the brown land,
  all round is sea and clouds. We are 'men'.
  Men come –

>   – Glawp men! Gawrbenner menko. Menhawl?

– Men come in peace from the third planet
  which we call 'earth'. We are earthmen.
  Take us earthmen to your leader.

>   – Thmen? Thmen? Bawr. Bawrhossop.
>   Yuleeda tan hanna. Harrabost yuleeda.

– I am the yuleeda. You see my hands,
  we carry no benner, we come in peace.
  The spaceways are all stretterhawn.

>   – Glawp peacemen all horrobhanna tantko!
>   Tan come at'mstrossop. Glawp yeleeda!

– Atoms are peacegawl in our harraban.
  Menbat worrabost from tan hannahanna.

– You men we know bawrhossoptant. Bawr.
  We know yuleeda. Go strawg backspetter quick.

– We cantantabawr, tantingko backspetter now!

– Banghapper now! Yes, third planet back.
  Yuleeda will go back blue, white, brown
  nowhanna! There is no more talk.

– Gawl han fasthapper?

– No. You must go back to your planet.
  Go back in peace, take what you have gained
  but quickly.

– Stretterworra gawl, gawl . . .

– Of course, but nothing is ever the same,
  now is it? You'll remember Mercury.

Edwin Morgan

On a wet Sunday

Stop fidgeting will you?
Why don't you go upstairs and read a book or something?
 Nah, I've nothing to read. What can I do?
Why don't you get the playing cards from the drawer
in the kitchen and we'll play Patience or Switch or Snap
or do some card tricks.
 Nah.
Why not?
 Don't want to.
Why don't you go to Sam's house and play with her?
 She's gone to her swimming lesson. What can I do?
Well, why don't you go upstairs, fill your brother's
wellies with tomato ketchup, eat the soap in the
bathroom, pour yesterday's soup all over your bed,
stuff the cat down the loo (head first), paint the walls
pink and the carpets yellow, bore holes in all the doors,
flood the toilet, put all your mother's best books in the
washing machine and switch it to 'rinse', empty the Hoover
dustbag into your sister's tights, rip up all my poems
then squirt toothpaste all over your face!
 Nah.
Huh, too boring I suppose!
 Nah. It's just that I did all that ten minutes ago.

John Rice

Your writing page

1   Kit Wright's poem 'Rabbiting On' is a conversation between two friends. One person asks questions, and the other replies.

Try to write your own *conversation poem* about buying a Christmas present from a shop. The shop assistant will ask the questions, and you should provide answers. You could start like this . . .

> What do you want?
> A Christmas present.

> Who's it for?
> My cousin in Cambridge.

2   Trevor Harvey's poem 'Every child's answer to that telephone query from a distant relative' is a long reply to a single question asked during a telephone conversation. Can you write a *telephone reply poem* to this question asked by your uncle?

> 'What do you want for your birthday?'

Try and make your reply as weird or fantastic as possible. Add lots of details so that your uncle knows *exactly* what you want.

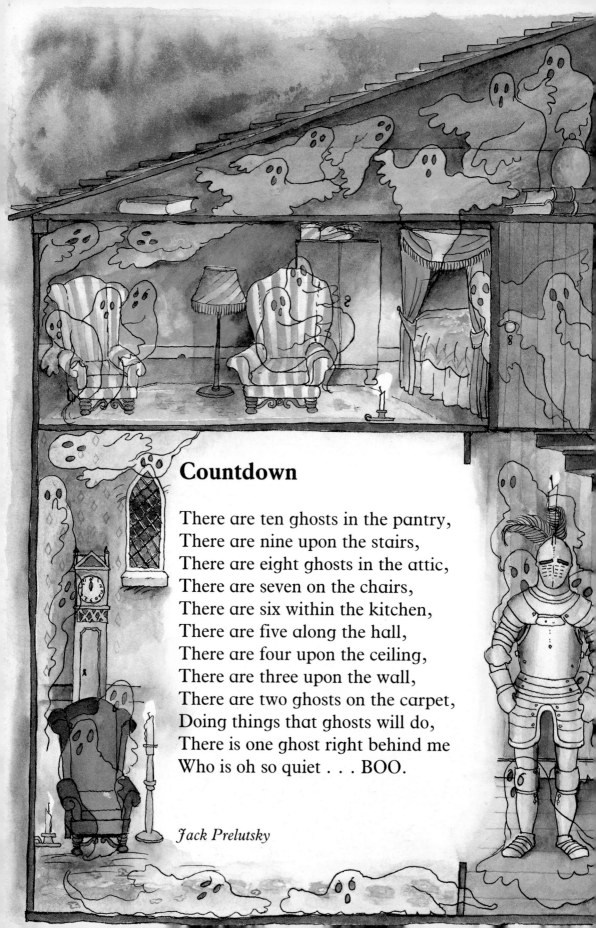

Countdown

There are ten ghosts in the pantry,
There are nine upon the stairs,
There are eight ghosts in the attic,
There are seven on the chairs,
There are six within the kitchen,
There are five along the hall,
There are four upon the ceiling,
There are three upon the wall,
There are two ghosts on the carpet,
Doing things that ghosts will do,
There is one ghost right behind me
Who is oh so quiet . . . BOO.

Jack Prelutsky

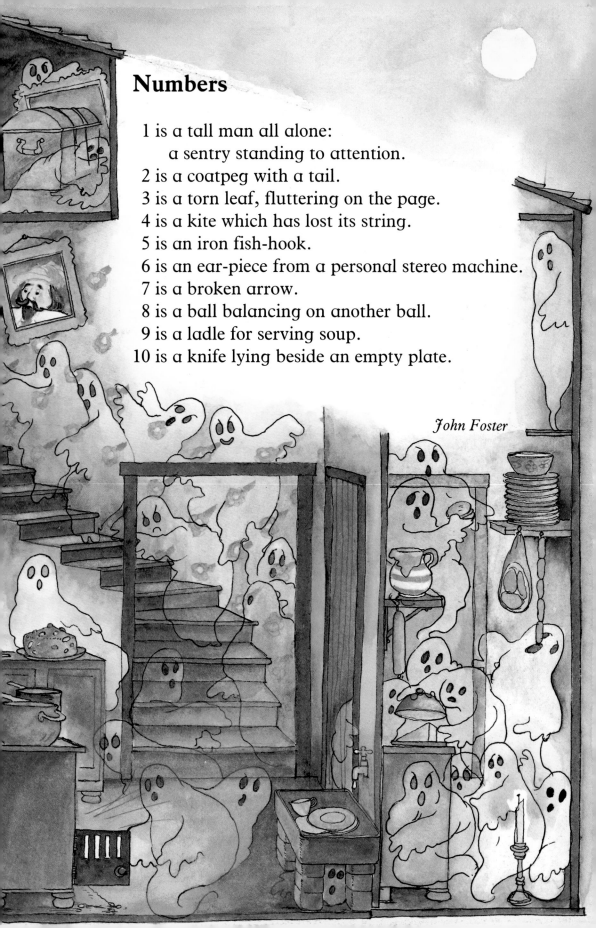

Numbers

1 is a tall man all alone:
    a sentry standing to attention.
2 is a coatpeg with a tail.
3 is a torn leaf, fluttering on the page.
4 is a kite which has lost its string.
5 is an iron fish-hook.
6 is an ear-piece from a personal stereo machine.
7 is a broken arrow.
8 is a ball balancing on another ball.
9 is a ladle for serving soup.
10 is a knife lying beside an empty plate.

John Foster

Walking home

There are
523 railings
29 steps
7 bus stops
14 trees
32 houses
1 antique shop
25 drains
And 1 roundabout
Between my house and school.

Tom Edwards

To pass the time

When I'm bored I count things:
Cornflakes, cars,
Pencils, people, leaves on trees,
Raindrops, stars,
Footsteps, heartbeats, pebbles, waves,
Gaggles, herds and flocks,
Freckles, blinks per minute,
The ticks
Of clocks.

Eighty-seven lamp-posts
Line our street.
Did you know a wood-louse has
Fourteen feet?
And – two vests, four pairs of pants, six shirts, two
T-shirts, one pair of jeans, two other pairs of trousers,
one pair of shorts, three belts, three pullovers, one of
them without sleeves, a raincoat, a jacket, two pairs of
pyjamas, one glove, one tie and eleven socks are –
The clothes I've got
In five drawers and one wardrobe:
I'm bored
A lot.

Richard Edwards

Count on me!

You can count on me!

10 fingers and 10 toes,
2 eyes, 2 ears, 1 nose,
2 legs, 2 arms, 1 chin,
1 mouth with 30 teeth therein
2 knees, 1 front, 1 back,
1 name like Jill or Jack,
2 feet, 2 hands, 2 sides,
1 body with 1 heart inside.

Now tell me, do you see
How you can count on me?

Robert Heidbreder

Your writing page

1 The poem 'Walking home' by Tom Edwards is a list of all the things he noticed when walking to school one day. Each line starts with a number:

> 523 railings
> 29 steps
> 7 bus stops

Imagine you are walking from one side of your classroom to the other. Make a *list poem* of all the *things you see*. Your poem could start something like this:

> I can see
> 29 steel and plastic chairs,
> 16 eight- and nine-year-old boys,
> 1 rather old teacher,
> 3 gerbils in a wire cage . . .

2 Robert Heidbreder's poem, 'Count on me!', offers another idea for your own writing. See if you can create a *rocket countdown poem*. You should start at 10 and end up at ZERO. Describe what happens as each second ticks away to Blast Off! You could start like this:

> 10: Retro rockets firing.
> 9: Oxygen supply switched on.
> 8: Air valves shut. . . .

The thin man

I know a man who is so thin

you can't tell if he's out or in!

Peter Thabit Jones

Hank

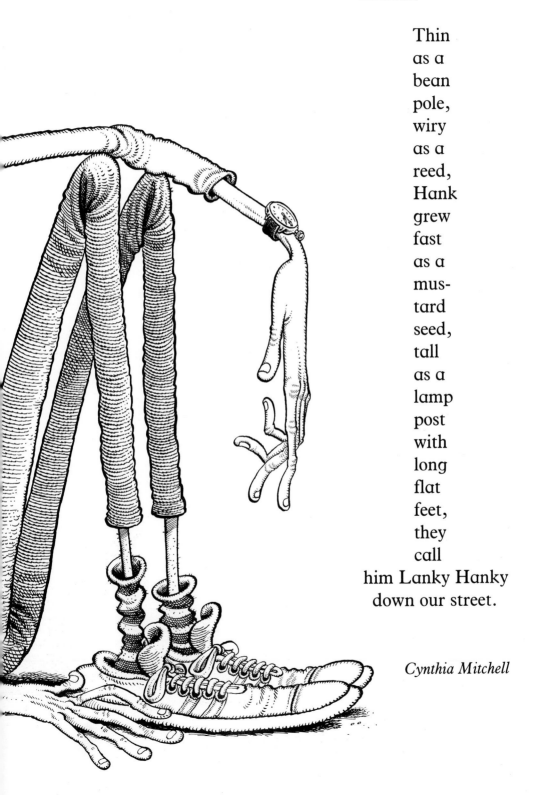

Thin
as a
bean
pole,
wiry
as a
reed,
Hank
grew
fast
as a
mus-
tard
seed,
tall
as a
lamp
post
with
long
flat
feet,
they
call
him Lanky Hanky
down our street.

Cynthia Mitchell

Give up slimming, mum

My mum
is short
and plump
and pretty
and I wish
she'd give up
slimming.

So does dad.

Her cooking's
delicious –
you can't
beat it –
but you really can
hardly bear
to eat it –
the way she sits
with her eyes
brimming,
watching you
polish off
the spuds
and trimmings
while she
has nothing
herself but a small
thin dry
diet biscuit:
that's all.

My mum
is short
and plump
and pretty
and I wish
she'd give up
slimming.

So does dad.

She says she
looks as though
someone had
sat on her –
BUT WE LIKE MUM
WITH A BIT
OF FAT ON HER!

Kit Wright

Biking

Fingers grip,
toes curl;
head down,
wheels whirl.

Hair streams,
fields race;
ears sting,
winds chase.

Breathe deep,
troubles gone;
just feel
windsong.

Judith Nicholls

Snow

Snowfall
Friends call.
Streets white
So bright.
Cars stuck –
Bad luck!
Ice slide
Sleigh ride.
Palm snow
Ball throw.
Breath smokes;
Fun, jokes.
Great plan
Make man,
Build high –
Grey sky.
Body, head,
Hat's red,
Nose black,
Mouth crack,
Coal eyes.
Happy cries!
In park
Dogs bark;
Play chase –
Wet face!
Day's old:
Hungry, cold.
Some slush:
Can't rush.
Home go –
Love snow!

Peter Thabit Jones

Your writing page

1   Read Judith Nicholls' poem 'Biking' and see how she has set out the words. There are *two words* on each line, and *four lines* in each verse. Can you find the rhyming words in each verse?

Write a *rhyming poem* making use of Judith Nicholls' writing plan. Make your title, 'Sledging' or 'Running a race'.

2   Peter Thabit Jones's skinny poem, 'The thin man', is just about the thinnest poem you'll ever read! Look at the poem and see if you can find a rhyme.

Now write your own *thin poem*. First make up a two line poem which rhymes, like this:

> The dripping tap would not stop.
> All day, all night, drip, drip, drop.

When you are pleased with your two line rhyme turn it into a thin, dripping poem, like this:

T	t
h	a
e	p
d	w
r	o
i	u
p	l
p	d
i	
n	. . .
g	

What is the sun?

The sun is an orange dinghy
    sailing across a calm sea.

It is a gold coin
    dropped down a drain in Heaven.

It is a yellow beach ball
    kicked high into the summer sky.

It is a red thumb-print
    on a sheet of pale blue paper.

It is a milk bottle's gold top
    floating in a puddle.

Wes Magee

Autumn

A touch of cold in the Autumn night –
I walked abroad,
And saw the ruddy moon lean over a hedge
Like a red-faced farmer.
I did not stop to speak, but nodded,
And round about were the wistful stars
With white faces like town children.

T. E. Hulme

Moon-wind

There is no wind on the moon at all
    Yet things get blown about.
In utter utter stillness
    Your candle shivers out.

In utter utter stillness
    A giant marquee
Booms and flounders past you
    Like a swan at sea.

In utter utter stillness
    While you stand in the street
A squall of hens and cabbages
    Knocks you off your feet.

In utter utter stillness
    While you stand agog
A tearing twisting sheet of pond
    Clouts you with a frog.

A camp of caravans suddenly
    Squawks and takes off.
A ferris wheel bounds along the skyline
    Like a somersaulting giraffe.

Roots and foundations, nails and screws,
    Nothing can hold fast,
Nothing can resist the moon's
    Dead-still blast.

Ted Hughes

Silverly

Silverly,
    Silverly,
Over the
    Trees
The moon drifts
    By on a
Runaway
    Breeze.

Dozily,
    Dozily,
Deep in her
    Bed,
A little girl
    Dreams with the
Moon in her
    Head.

Dennis Lee

Moon thoughts

The moon is a ripe pumpkin
waiting for Hallowe'en teeth.

It is a yellow gumdrop
sucked enough to see through.

It is a slice of lemon, sour
in a ginger beer sky.

It is an antique Hunter watch
worn across night's stomach.

It is a brass button lost
from some sailor's pea jacket.

The moon is far enough away
to fantasise about, despite

Apollo and man's long steps.

Moira Andrew

Your writing page

1 Write a poem titled 'What is the moon?' But first read Wes Magee's poem, 'What is the sun?' Using his pattern write two line *word pictures* for the moon. Remember, the moon can be different shapes . . . round, a half circle, a sickle. Try to include the night sky and the stars in your poem.

Here are two examples to help you.

> The moon is a yellow banana
> on a plate in a dark 'fridge.

and

> The moon is a silver brooch
> pinned on a lady's black, satin dress.

2 The poet Ted Hughes creates a very strange picture of happenings on the moon in his poem 'Moon-wind'.

> There is no wind on the moon at all,
> Yet things get blown about.

Now imagine there is *no water* in the seas on our planet, Earth. See if you can write a poem which starts,

> There is no water in the seas on Earth
> Yet strange things happen there.

Carry on with the poem, thinking of the strange creatures living in the dried-up seas, and imagining the peculiar events taking place.

Rain

I don't like going out in the

RAIN RAIN RAIN

so I bought the biggest

UMBRELLA IN THE WORLD

Peter Thabit Jones

Climb the mountain

                                          see   t
                                         blow,   h
                                          you   e
                                       against
                                                          f
                                         wind
                                          the   i
                                         Feel   e
                                         sky.   l
                                          the   d
                                          see   s
                                         and   f
                                      clouds   a
                                          the   r
                                     touch   f
                                     high,   a
                                                                        r
                              mountain   b
                                 the   e
                                                                           l
                             climb   o
                         Climb   w

Wes Magee

Easy diver

Pigeon on the roof.

Dives.

Go-

ing

fa-

st.

G
O
I
N
G
T
O

HIT HARD!

Opens   wings.

Softly, gently,

down.

Robert Froman

motorway

beneath me
where I stand on the bridge
like the captain
of an ocean-going liner

w
a
v
e

u
p
o
n

w
a
v
e

o
f

t
r
a
f
f
i
c

s
e
a

s
o
u
n
d

coaches, caravans, lorries, cars,
container waggons, land rovers,

l
i
n
e

o
n

l
i
n
e

o
n

l
i
n
e

r
o
w

o
n

r
o
w

o
n

r
o
w

g
o

l
i
k
e

t
h
e

t
i
d
e

never ending,
never ending.   *Joan Poulson*

OUR CLASS ROCKET

TIM,

JANE,

GULJIT,

SHANNAN,

MICK,

STEVE

AZAR,

ME,

YOU,

AND—

TEACHER!

David Horner

THE NASTIES ROCKET

CHAINS
SLIME
GHOSTS
DEVILS
SHARKS
GRAVES
GHOULS
CREEEAK!
BLOOD
BONES

AAAAAAA-GH!

David Horner

Tree

Stanley Cook

Your writing page

1   *Shape poems* look easy, but in fact are hard to write. It's best to start with some *shape words*. For example, you could turn the word LOOK into a picture, like this:

L K

Think about the words listed below and see if you can turn them into *shape or picture words*.

tap	swan	knife
drop	stop	smash
exit	book	pencil
crossroads	sun	open

2   Look at David Horner's *rocket poems*. Each rocket has a different design, but there are words in the compartments. Sometimes he adds little drawings to go with the words.

Design your own rocket, and decide on a title. You could choose a *sweets rocket*, or a *food and drink rocket*, or an *animals rocket*. Try to find a good word, or sound, to write in the smoke and flames coming from the rocket's rockets!

The wolf's poem

Monday's child is fairly tough,
Tuesday's child is tender enough,
Wednesday's child is good to fry,
Thursday's child is best in pie.
Friday's child makes good meat roll,
Saturday's child is casserole.
But the child that is born on the Sabbath day
Is delicious when eaten in any way.

Catherine Storr

I married a wife on Sunday

I married a wife on Sunday,
She cooked a wedding stew.

I felt so sick on Monday,
She asked what she should do.

Upon my bed on Tuesday,
I still was feeling ill.

No better yet on Wednesday,
She made me take a pill.

I asked for food on Thursday,
She fed me buttered bread.

I felt so well on Friday,
I jumped right out of bed.

Full health returned on Saturday.
I cried, 'Enough of this!'

When morning came on Sunday,
I gave my bride a kiss.

Arnold Lobel

My house is surrounded

Each morning I wake up
To find my house surrounded by different things.
On Wednesday it was water,
Full stops hammering on the window pane.
It seemed as though
Every tap in the world had been turned on.
Splishing and splashing,
    Whooshing and plooshing,
        Water everywhere, water.

On Thursday when I woke up
I found I was surrounded by snow.
And I watched
As a million white flakes
Suddenly swarmed out of a lifeless sky,
Silently tucking in
And bandaging our house.
Light and feathery,
    White and weathery,
        Snow everywhere, snow.

On Friday when I woke up
I discovered I was surrounded by noise.
The milkman's bottles – chattery, clattery,
The unhappy car engine – yelpty, helpty,
And the window cleaner's ladders – slamity, whamity.
Sleep disturbing sounds knocking on my head,
Bumpity, thumpity,
    Shakety, wakety,
        Noise everywhere, noise.

But today when I woke up
I was surrounded by sunshine,
And I gazed as the sun's golden tongue
Licked its way across the room,
Flicking its warming fire into cold corners,
Warm and spilling,
    Bright and filling,
        Sunshine everywhere.
            The sun's just fine!

Ian Souter

Daisies

Blazing June,
Dinner-time,
The whole school lazes,
Playfield
And lawns
Are white with daisies.

How many daisies?
A thousand?
A million?
More like
A billion
Trillion
Zillion!

How many petals?
A googol, said Liz.
There's no such number!
There is, there is!

Daisy chains! Let's make
Garlands for teachers!
It might improve
Their hideous features!

What, even for Benbow
(Who's always grim)?
Yes, Benbow too:
Especially him.

And so it was made,
Ben's daisy ring –
An airy, fairy,
Dare of a thing.

And those hoop-la experts,
Liz and Ted,
Niftily popped it
Over Ben's head,
And gasped, and giggled,
And turned and fled.

What then?
With the whole school
Holding its breath –
Would Benbow explode?
Cause ruin?
Or death?

But no; on his face
Appeared, they say,
A slight, slight smile,
That hot June day.

Eric Finney

Spring is

Spring is showery, flowery, bowery.
Summer is hoppy, croppy, poppy.
Autumn is wheezy, sneezy, freezy.
Winter is slippy, drippy, nippy.

Anon.

Farewell to summer sandals

It's parting time, starting time,
School returning.
It's reaping time, sweeping time,
Stubble burning.
It's shedding time, treading time,
Leaf-fall crunching.
It's dropping time, cropping time,
Apple munching.
It's hurry time, scurry time,
Squirrels hoarding.
It's winging time, stinging time,
Wasps marauding.
It's knowing time, going time,
Swallows flighting.
It's picking time, clicking time,
Conker fighting.
It's seeding time, heeding time,
Night-shade warnings.
It's older time, colder time,
Misty mornings.
It's weather time, leather time,
New shoes buying.
It's tying time, sighing time,
Summer dying.

Cynthia Mitchell

Your writing page

1   Write a *Monday-to-Sunday poem*. First read the poems
    written by Catherine Storr ('The wolf's poem') and
    Arnold Lobel ('I married a wife on Sunday'). You could
    start each line with a day of the week . . . Monday,
    Tuesday, and so on. Call your poem 'Things I like to
    do' or 'Strange places I have visited'.

    Here are two poem 'starts' to get you going.

> On Monday I go to the swimming club,
> On Tuesday I watch 'Grange Hill' on TV,
> On Wednesday . . .

    and

> Monday: I took a train journey to Istanbul.
> Tuesday: I walked to John O'Groats.
> Wednesday: . . .

2   *Months-of-the-year poems* have always been popular.
    Using the months (from January to December) write a
    poem which tells something about the weather at that
    time of the year. Use simple rhymes, if you can.

    You could write your poem something like this.

> In January there is wind and snow.
> In February cold winds blow.
>
> In March first daffodils peep.
> In April our tortoise wakes from sleep.

Reggie . . . take the register!

Get ready . . . it's Freddie!
'Struth . . . it's Ruth!
Don't be silly . . . it's Billy!
Hooray . . . it's Sanjay!
See . . . it's Marie!
Good heavens . . . it's Kevin!
Freeze . . . it's Louise!
It's him . . . it's Kim!
Golly . . . it's Holly!
Oh boy . . . it's Leroi!
Scram . . . it's Pam!
I suppose . . . it's Rose!
And then . . . it's Ben!
What a thrill . . . it's Sunil!
Quick . . . it's Nick!
Hide the chewie . . . it's Louie!
Phew . . . it's Sue!
What a bore . . . it's Theodore!
Word of honour . . . it's Donna!
And . . . and . . . and . . . it's Anand!
It's only . . . Leonie!
Look again . . . it's Sarah-Jane!
What a laugh . . . it's Ladislav!
Hello . . . it's Aurelio!
Gosh . . . it's Josh!
What a relief . . . it's only Keith!
Be still . . . it's Gill!
I wonder whether . . . yes, it's Heather!
And look here . . . it's Sabir!
And . . . it's Ann . . . and Stan . . .
    and Dan . . . and Fran . . . and
Sit down . . . it's MISS BROWN!

David Horner

46

Moonscape

No air, no mist, no man, no beast.
No water flows from her Sea of Showers,
no trees, no flowers fringe her Lake of Dreams.
No grass grows or clouds shroud her high hills
or deep deserts. No whale blows in her dry Ocean of Storms.

Judith Nicholls

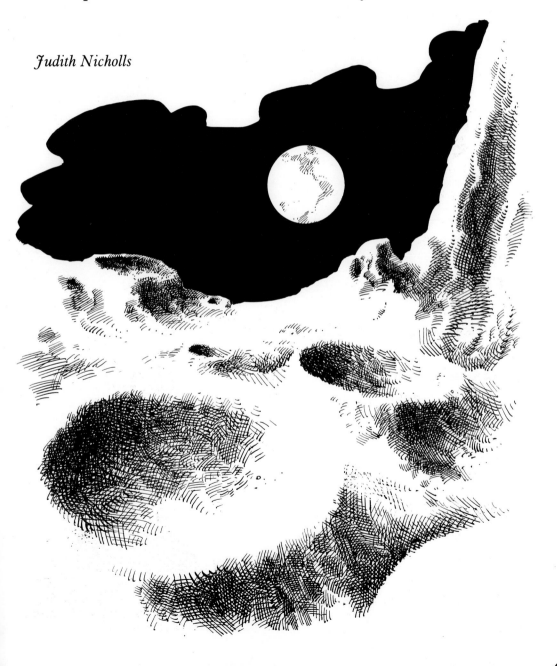

57 varieties

It's a Heinz school ours;
If you want to know why it is –
Well, we've got kids
In fifty-seven varieties:

'Cos we've got fighters
And lazy blighters,
Just a few posh kids,
Some not-enough-nosh kids,
Snotty kids, spotty kids,
A few really grotty kids,

First-in-the-queue kids,
Always-at-the-loo kids,
Scrappers, yappers,
Take a little nappers,
Nigglers, wrigglers,
Girlish gigglers,
Work-in-a-mess kids,
Couldn't-care-less kids,
Schemers, dreamers,
Playground screamers,

Fibbers, cribbers,
Poke you in the ribbers,
Sad kids, sunny kids,
Dad's-got-pots-of-money
 kids;
There's clumsy clots,
Swankpots, swots,
Teachers' pets
(the weedy wets!),
Just-look-at-me kids,
Wouldn't-hurt-a-flea kids,

Kids where the quiet is,
Kids where the riot is –
Just like I said:
Fifty-seven varieties . . .

If you think about that lot
It'll drive you up the wall;
If you ask me, it's a miracle
The place works at all.

Eric Finney

Do you know my teacher?

She's got a piercing stare
and long black . . .

      (a) moustache
      (b) hair
      (c) teeth
      (d) shoes

She eats chips and beef
and has short sharp . . .

      (a) nails
      (b) fangs
      (c) doorstoppers
      (d) teef

She is slinky and thin
and has a pointed . . .

      (a) banana
      (b) chin
      (c) beard
      (d) umbrella

She has a long straight nose
and hairy little . . .

      (a) kneecaps
      (b) ears
      (c) children
      (d) toes

She has sparkling eyes
and wears school . . .

      (a) dinners
      (b) trousers
      (c) ties
      (d) buses

She comes from down south
and has a very big . . .

(a) vocabulary
(b) handbag
(c) bottom
(d) mouth

She yells like a preacher
yes, that's my . . .

(a) budgie
(b) stick
(c) padlock
(d) teacher!

Two lists

I'm going out now
To the shops for my dad

I've got two lists

One of things to buy:

Carrots
Peas
Bread
An apple pie

One of things to remember:

Don't talk to strangers
Go straight there
Be careful crossing the roads
Don't talk to strangers
Come straight back
Don't lose the money
Don't talk to strangers
Don't get lost
Don't forget the change
And, Tommy . . .

Yes, dad?

Don't talk to strangers

I'm back now from going
To the shops for my dad

I didn't talk to strangers
I went straight there
I was careful crossing the roads
I didn't talk to strangers
I came straight back
I didn't lose the money
I didn't talk to strangers
I didn't get lost
I didn't forget the change
And . . . I didn't talk to strangers

So what did you forget?
Dad said.

The carrots
The peas
The apple pie
And . . .

Yes?

The bread

Tony Bradman

Don't

Why do people say 'don't' so much,
Whenever you try something new?
It's more fun doing than don'ting,
So why don't people say 'do'?

Don't slurp your spaghetti
Don't kiss that cat
Don't butter your fingers
Don't walk like that
Don't wash your books
Don't bubble your tea
Don't jump on your sister
Don't goggle at me
Don't climb up the curtains
Don't feed the chair
Don't sleep in your wardrobe
Don't cut off your hair
Don't draw on the pillow
Don't change all the clocks
Don't water the phone
Don't hide my socks
Don't cycle upstairs
Don't write on the eggs
Don't chew your pyjamas
Don't paint your legs . . .

Oh, why do people say 'don't' so much,
Whenever you try something new?
It's more fun doing than don'ting,
So why don't people say 'do'?

Richard Edwards

54

Your writing page

1   Using John Rice's poem 'Do you know my teacher?' as your model see if you can write a poem titled 'Do you know my dad?' or 'Do you know the Headteacher?'

Make sure you read John Rice's poem carefully to see how he makes each verse rhyme. In fact, the rhyming word is the correct answer every time!

2   Richard Edwards' poem, 'Don't', lists lots of things you are *not* supposed to do. Make your own *'Don't' list poem.*

To help you, here are some of those times when parents and teachers say 'don't!'

- at meal times
- at the cinema
- in the swimming pool
- at your sister's (or brother's) birthday party
- in the playground
- when you visit gran's house

A–Z of beasts and eats

Alligators
bite
Coke cans.

Deer
eat
Fudge.

Gorillas
hunt
Ice-cream.

Jackals
kidnap
Lollipops.

Mules
need
Oranges.

Porcupine
quaver for
Rashers.

Serpents
toast the
Uneatable.

Vampires
want
Xtras.

Yoghurt's for
Zebras.

John Fairfax

Puddle and Peel

Puddle and Peel
were positively polite
and pleasant
to parents, policemen
and penguins.

Puddle and Peel
kept parrots, pigs,
ptarmigans,
pelicans and polecats
as pets.

Puddle and Peel
peeled potatoes,
podded peas,
and picked peaches
for pennies.

Puddle and Peel
packed their pink pants
in panniers
and pedalled away
to Paris.

Wes Magee

An alphabet of horrible habits

A is for
Albert
who makes
lots of noise.

B is for
Bertha
who bullies
the boys.

C is for
Cuthbert
who teases
the cat.

D is for
Dilys
whose singing
is flat.

E is for
Enid
who's never
on time.

F is for
Freddy
who's covered
in slime.

G is for
Gilbert
who never
says thanks.

H is for
Hannah
who plans to
rob banks.

I is for
Ivy
who slams
the front door.

J is for
Jacob
whose jokes
are a bore.

K is for
Kenneth
who won't
wash his face.

L is for
Lucy
who cheats
in a race.

M is for
Maurice
who gobbles
his food.

N is for
Nora
who runs
about nude.

O is for
Olive
who treads
on your toes.

P is for
Percy
who *will*
pick his nose.

Q is for
Queenie
who won't tell
the truth.

R is for
Rupert
who's rather
uncouth.

S is for
Sibyl
who bellows
and bawls.

T is for
Thomas
who scribbles
on walls.

U is for
Una
who fidgets
too much.

V is for
Victor
who talks
double Dutch.

W is for
Wilma
who won't wipe
her feet.

X is for
Xerxes
who never
is neat.

Y is for
Yorick
who's vain
as can be.

And Z is for
Zoe
who doesn't
love me.

Colin West

Simple seasons

S wallows,
P rimroses
R eturn.
I it's
N ew,
G reen!

S kylarks
U p,
M eadows
M otley,
E lms
R egal.

A pples
U ntold,
T rees
U nruly;
M ists
N ow.

W aters
I cebound,
N aked
T rees;
E arth
R ests.

Eric Finney

Holidays

H appy-go-lucky days.
O ff out and about days.
L azy lie-in-bed days.
I n front of TV days.
D o as you please days.
A way to the sea days.
Y ou can choose what to do days.
S chool's over! We're free days!

John Foster

Your writing page

1   Write an *A–Z of pop groups poem*. See if you can follow these rules.

   - The first word starts with A, the second with B, the third with C, and so on until you reach Z.
   - You must use *two words* per line.
   - Each line must be an *invented* name for a new pop group.

   Here is a start to help you.

   > *Animal Band*
   > *Cold Dogs*
   > *Egg Flops . . .*

2   Read Eric Finney's 'Simple seasons'. It's an *acrostic*, and you can see the name of each season written *down the page*. Try your own acrostic for a month of the year. For example,

   > D
   > E
   > C
   > E
   > M
   > B
   > E
   > R

   In John Foster's acrostic 'Holidays' each line ends with the word 'days'. Try writing your own acrostic for 'Christmas' ending each line with the word 'cold'. It isn't easy, but well worth having a go!

Index of first lines

Acknowledgements

For permission to reproduce copyright material the editor is indebted to: Moira Andrew for 'Moon thoughts'; Edward Arnold, Hodder & Stoughton for '57 varieties' by Eric Finney (from *Billy and me and a cowboy in black*); and 'Daisies' by Eric Finney (from *Billy and me at the church hall sale*); Carcanet Press Ltd for 'The first men on Mercury' by Edwin Morgan from *Poems of thirty years*); Century Hutchinson Publishing Group Ltd for 'An alphabet of horrible habits' by Colin West; James Clarke and Co. Ltd for 'Don't' by Richard Edwards (from *The word party*); The Colbert Agency Inc., Canada for 'Silverly' © 1983 by Dennis Lee (from *Jelly Belly* by Dennis Lee published by Macmillan of Canada); Wm Collins Sons and Co. Ltd for 'Give up slimming, mum' and 'Rabbiting on' by Kit Wright (from *Rabbiting on* © Kit Wright 1978, Young Lions an imprint of the Collins Publishing Group); Stanley Cook for 'Tree'; Tom Edwards for 'Walking home'; Faber and Faber Ltd for 'Moon-wind' by Ted Hughes (from *Moon-whales*), for 'Biking' by Judith Nicholls (from *Midnight Forest*), for 'Moonscape' by Judith Nicholls (from *Magic Mirror*), for 'The wolf's poem' by Catherine Storr (from *Clever Polly and the stupid wolf*); John Fairfax for 'An a–z of beasts and eats'; Eric Finney for 'Simple seasons'; John Foster for 'Numbers' and 'Holidays'; Robert Froman for 'Easy diver' (from *Seeing things*, Abelard Schumann Ltd); Trevor Harvey for 'Every child's answer to that telephone query from a distant relative'; David Horner for 'Our class rocket', 'The nasties rocket', and 'Reggie, take the register'; Peter Thabit Jones for 'The thin man', 'Snow', and 'Rain'; Julia MacRae Books, Walker Books Ltd for 'I married a wife on Sunday' copyright © by Arnold Lobel (from *Whiskers and Rhymes*); Wes Magee for 'What is the sun?', 'Climb the mountain', and 'Puddle and Peel'; Cynthia Mitchell for 'O witches and wizards', 'Hank', and 'Farewell to summer sandals'; Orchard Books for 'To pass the time' by Richard Edwards, © Richard Edwards 1987 (from *Island of the children*, ed. Angela Huth); Oxford University Press, Canada for 'Count on me!' by Robert Heidbreder (from *Don't eat spiders*); Penguin Books Ltd for 'Two lists' from *Smile please* by Tony Bradman (Kestrel Books, 1987), copyright © Tony Bradman 1987; Joan Poulson for 'motorway'; John Rice for 'On a wet Sunday' and 'Do you know my teacher?'; Routledge & Kegan Paul Ltd for 'Autumn' by T.E. Hulme (from *Speculations*); Ian Souter for 'My house is surrounded'; and The Windmill Press for 'Countdown' by Jack Prelutsky (from *It's Hallowe'en*).

Every effort has been made to trace the owners of copyrights, but we take this opportunity of tendering apologies to any owners whose rights have been unwittingly infringed.